A B C

READER

SMALL AND CAPITAL LETTERS

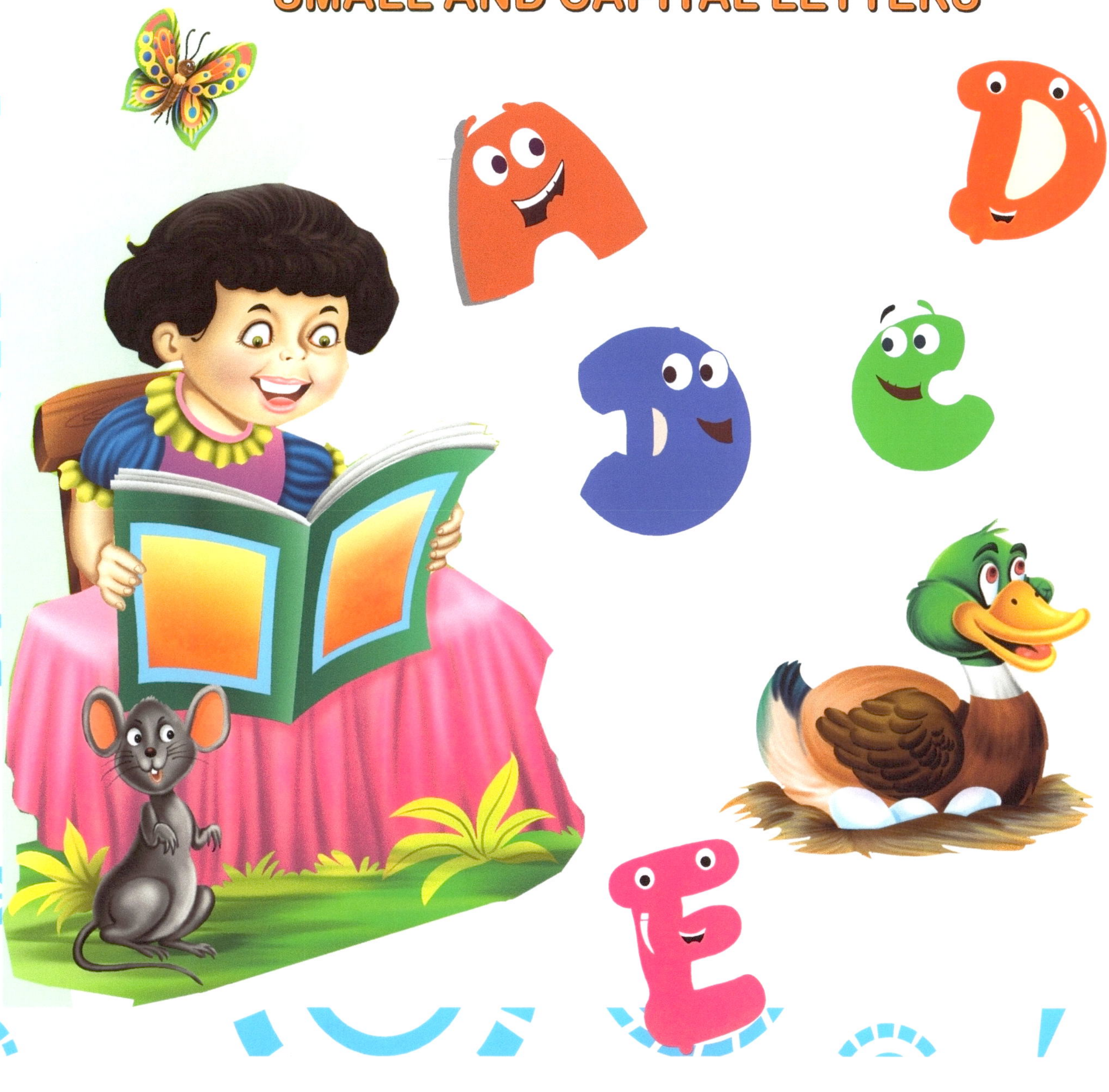

A
a
APPLE
Ant
Aeroplane
Axe

B
b
BALL
Bat
Balloon
Bag

C
C
CAT
Candle
Clown
Cake

D d

DOG

Dolphin **D**inosaur **D**uck

E e

ELEPHANT

Egg

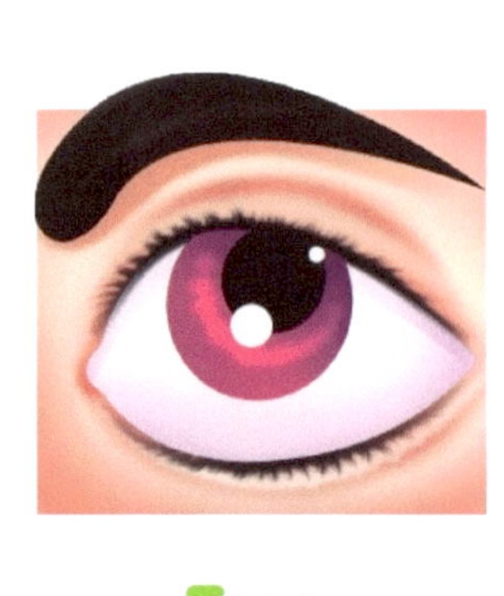

Eye

Eagle

H
h
HORSE
Helicopter
Hammer
Hen

I i

ICE-CREAM

Igloo
Iron
Island

J j

JOKER

Jam

Jar

Jeep

K
k
KITE
King
Kettle
Kangaroo

L l

LION

Lemon

Lock

Lamp

M m

MONKEY

Moon

Mango

Mask

N n

NEST

Nurse

Net

Newspaper

O

ORANGE

P
p
PARROT
Pea
Pear
Pencil

Q q

QUEEN

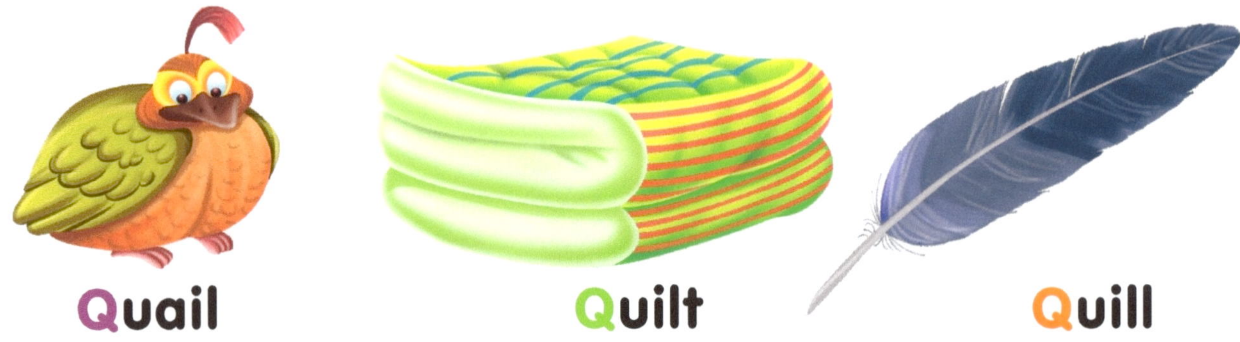

Quail

Quilt

Quill

R r

S
s
SHIP
Snake
Soap
Snail
20

T
t
TIGER
Telephone
Tomato
Turtle

U u

U UMBRELLA

Unicorn

Utensils

Uniform

V v

VAN

Violin

Vase

Volcano

W w

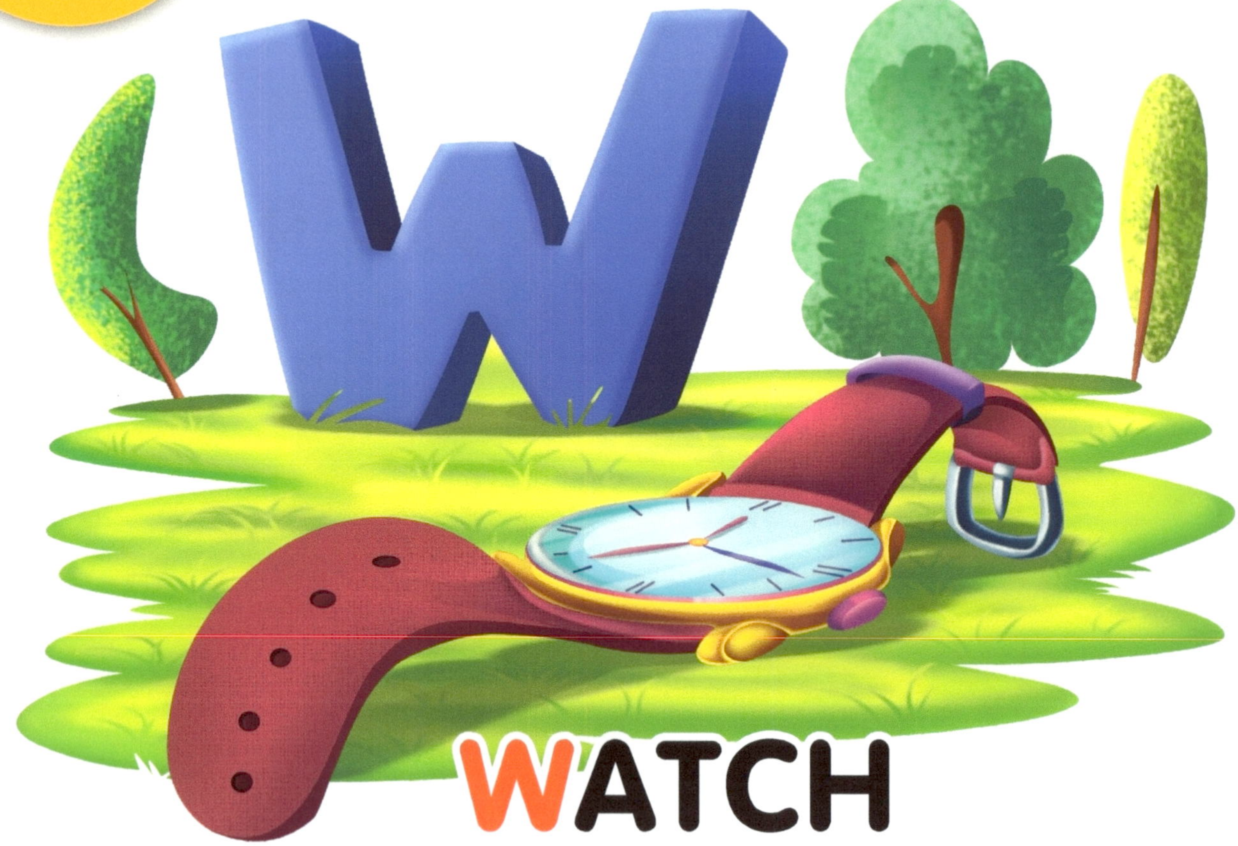

WATCH

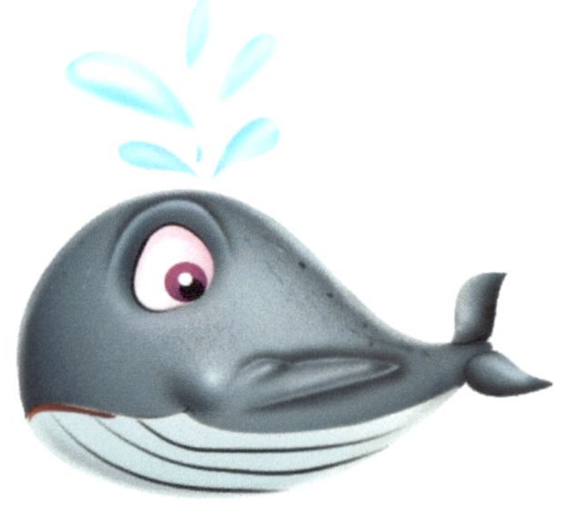

Whale

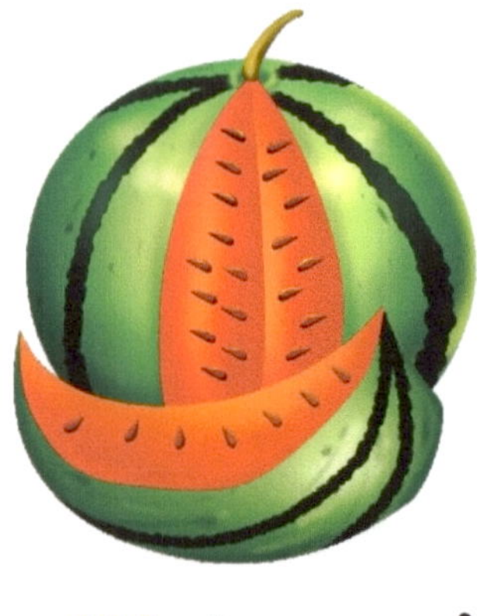

Watermelon

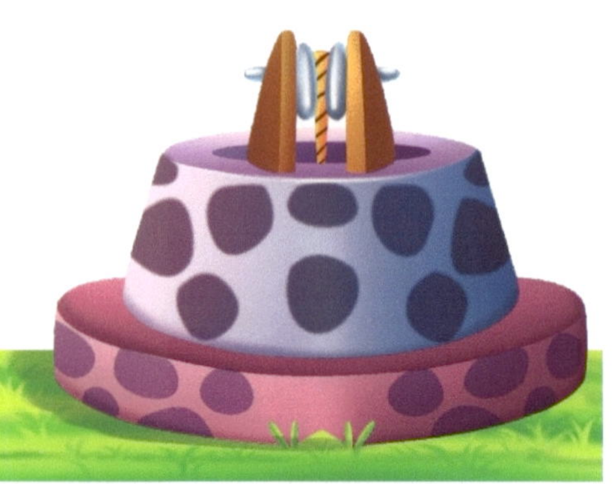

Well

X x

X-MAS TREE

X-ray

Xylophone

Xerox

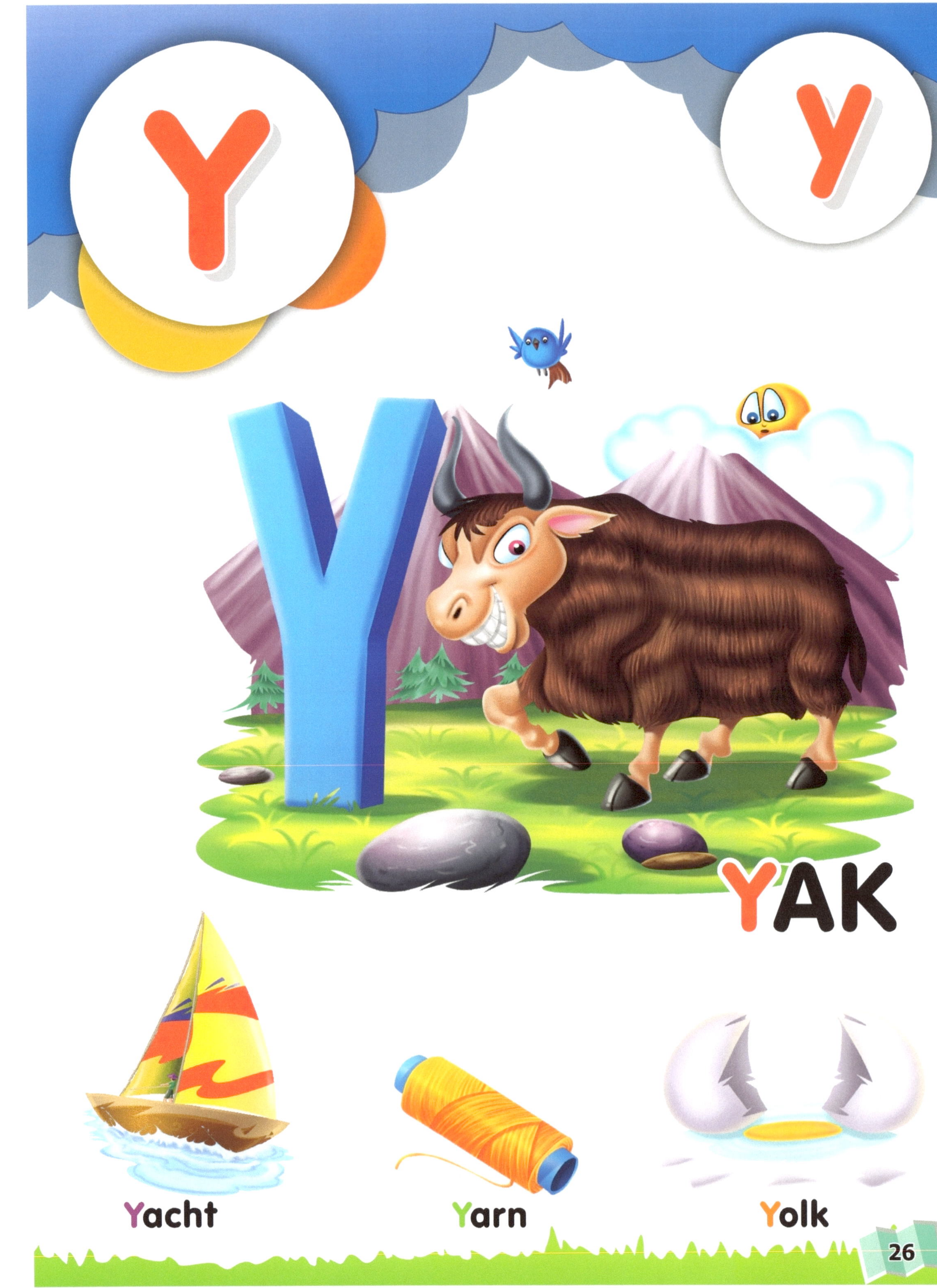

Y
y
YAK
Yacht
Yarn
Yolk

Z z

ZEBRA

Zoo

Zig-zag

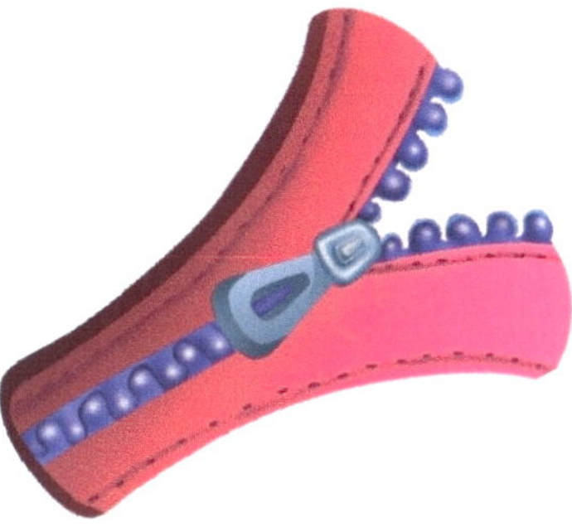

Zip

ALPHABET AT A GLANCE

 **A** for **APPLE**

 **B** for **BALL**

 **C** for **CAT**

 **D** for **DOG**

 **E** for **ELEPHANT**

 **F** for **FISH**

 **G** for **GRAPES**

 **H** for **HORSE**

 **I** for **ICE-CREAM**

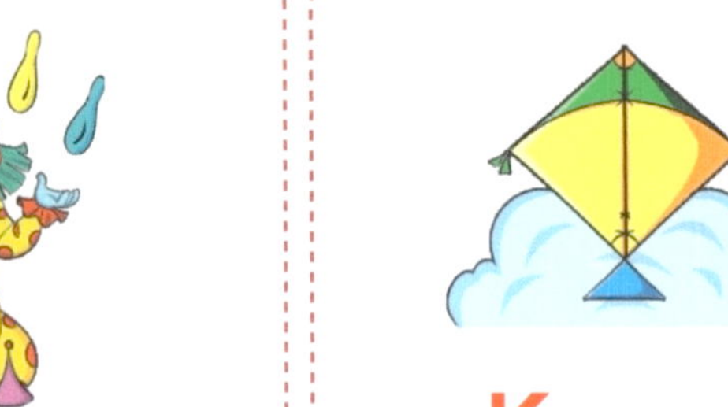 **J** for **JOKER**

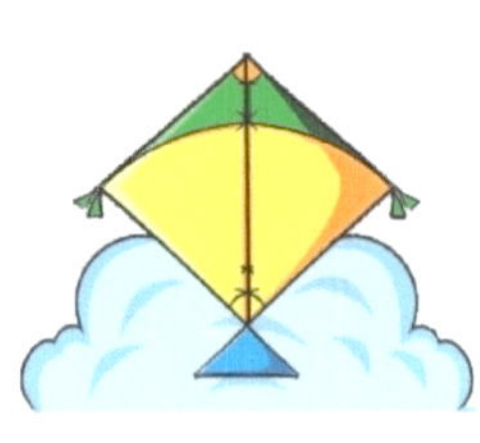 **K** for **KITE**

 **L** for **LION**

M for **MANGO**

N for NEST
O for ORANGE
P for PARROT
Q for QUEEN
R for RAT
S for SUN
T for TIGER
U for UMBRELLA
V for VEGETABLES
W for WATERMELON
X for XYLOPHONE
Y for YACHT
Z for ZEBRA

CAPITAL LETTERS

A B C D

E F G H

I J K L

M N O P

Q R S T

U V W X

Y Z

SMALL LETTERS

a b c d
e f g h
i j k l
m n o p
q r s t
u v w x
y z

ALPHABET SONG

Come little children
Come to me,
I will teach you ABC

ABCD, EFG
HIJK, LMNOP
LMNOP QRST,
UVW, XYZ

Butter on your bread
If you don't like
It's time to go to bed

www.ingramcontent.com/pod-product-compliance
Lightning Source LLC
Chambersburg PA
CBHW042116110726
48006CB00002B/660